EWAN McGREGOR

Julia Holt

Published in association with The Basic Skills Agency

Hodder & Stoughton

A MEMBER OF THE HODDER HEADLINE GROUP

Acknowledgements

Cover: © Graham Whitby Boot/Allstar

Photos: p 3 Graham Whitby Boot/Allstar; p 9 The Ronald Grant Archive; pp. 11, 15, Moviestore Collection; pp 19, 23, Michael Crabtree/Press Association/Topham; p 26 Tom Vickers/Press Association/Topham

Every effort has been made to trace copyright holders of material reproduced in this book. Any rights not acknowledged will be acknowledged in subsequent printings if notice is given to the publisher.

Orders; please contact Bookpoint Ltd, 39 Milton Park, Abingdon, Oxon OX14 4TD. Telephone: (44) 01235 400414, Fax: (44) 01235 400454. Lines are open from 9.00–6.00, Monday to Saturday, with a 24 hour message answering service.
Email address: orders@bookpoint.co.uk

British Library Cataloguing in Publication Data
A catalogue record for this title is available from the British Library

ISBN 0 340 77664 1

First published 2000
Impression number   10 9 8 7 6 5 4 3 2 1
Year   2005 2004 2003 2002 2001 2000

Copyright © 2000 Julia Holt

Typeset by GreenGate Publishing Services, Tonbridge, Kent.
Printed in Great Britain for Hodder and Stoughton Educational, a division of Hodder Headline Plc, 338 Euston Road, London NW1 3BH, by Redwood Books, Trowbridge, Wilts

Contents

1 The Beginning

One day in 1978
a six-year-old boy
was waiting for his Mum
to pick him up from school.
She was taking him to the cinema.
They were going to see *Star Wars*.
This was special.
Uncle Dennis was in it.

In fact Uncle Dennis
played a rebel fighter pilot
in the first three *Star Wars* films.
The little boy was very proud of his Uncle.
The little boy's name was Ewan McGregor.
He can still remember everything about that day.

Ewan's parents were teachers.
They lived in Crieff,
a small town in Scotland.
Crieff is famous
because Rob Roy MacGregor
had many fights there against the English.

At school in Crieff, Ewan was musical.
He played the French horn and the guitar.
He was also a good mimic.
He pretended to be Elvis for his friends.
At the age of five
he went on stage for the first time.
He played the Sheriff of Nottingham.

Ewan at the Cannes Film Festival in 1996.

By the age of nine
Ewan had made up his mind to be an actor.
Uncle Dennis was his hero.
When he came to visit their quiet town
he had long hair and wore beads.
Ewan wanted to be different like him.

As he got older, Ewan struggled at school.
He was good at music
but not very good at maths and English.
School was difficult for him.
His parents were teachers
and his older brother, Colin,
was good at everything.
Colin was Head Boy
and went on to be an RAF fighter pilot.
Ewan was always in trouble.

2 College Days

His parents were very understanding.
When he was sixteen they said,
'You can leave school if you want to'.
So he did.
With his Mum's help he got his first job.
He worked back stage
in a theatre in Perth.
He was paid £50 a week.

Ewan stayed there for six months.
Then in 1988 he went to college
to do an HNC in drama.
Even then his college friends saw
that he had talent.

In 1989 Ewan made up his mind
to study in London.
He was chosen from 700 others
to study at The Guildhall School
of Music and Drama.
He studied for three years
and fell in love with London.
He still lives there today.

At the start of their third year,
the Guildhall students put on a show.
They all hoped to be picked out by agents.
Sadly, when it came to Ewan's turn
he forgot his lines.

3 Ewan's First Part

Ewan's mistake did not put off one director.
She was casting a new TV series.
It was called *Lipstick On Your Collar*.
She asked Ewan to try out for a part.
He did his take-off of Elvis
and the part was his.
In 1992 he dropped out of college.

The six-part series
took seven months to make.
It was a good start to Ewan's career.
He played the part of a soldier
who dreams of being a rock and roll star.
Critics did not like the series
when it came out in 1993
but they did like Ewan.

Work was hard to find for the rest of 1992.
No one knew him as yet.
However, Ewan did get a trip to North Africa
for a one-line part in a film.
This gave him a chance to study filming.

When *Lipstick On Your Collar* came out
it got him a star part in another TV series.
It was a costume drama
called *Scarlet And Black*.
It was about a poor young Frenchman
who becomes a soldier and a hero.
The series had lots of love scenes.
At one point Ewan had to run naked
across a field.
Later he joked 'I've been naked
in almost everything I've done.
In fact I have it written in my contract.'

Ewan in a promotion for *Lipstick on your Collar*.

4 Ewan is a Hit!

Ten million people saw Ewan
in *Scarlet and Black*
and they loved it.
He soon had fan mail for the first time.

He had even more fans after his next film.
It was called *Shallow Grave*.
The film tells the story of three flatmates.
One night a man dies in their flat.
They have to get rid of the man's body
because they want to keep his money.
The film is a dark comedy.
To get into the mood
Ewan and his two co-stars shared a flat
before they started the 30-day filming.
It paid off, the film was a big hit.

Christopher Eccleston, Kerry Fox and Ewan in *Shallow Grave*.

Shallow Grave was even more successful
than its makers hoped.
It made £20 million and won an award
for the best British film of the year.
Ewan was said to be 'the next big thing'.

His next TV job didn't do much for his career
but he did meet a Frenchwoman called Eve.
She was a set designer.
They fell in love.

Blue Juice was Ewan's next film.
It was a surfing film
made in the cold winter months of 1994.
Blue Juice was not a hit film,
but Ewan and the cast had a great time making it.
He said, 'I've never partied so much
in all my life.'

At the very end of 1994
Ewan went to Japan
to make his oddest film yet.
In *The Pillow Book*
he plays an Englishman in Japan.
His lover writes on his skin
in Japanese.

It took four hours a day
for the make-up artists to write all over him.
Again, he was naked in the film.
He was worried about what his parents would think
but they said the film was very beautiful.

5 The Big Break

It was clear that Ewan was happy
to take risks with his work.
It was this talent
that gave him his big break
with the film *Trainspotting*.

The film was made by the same team
that made *Shallow Grave*
The 30 sets for *Trainspotting*
were built inside an old cigarette factory.
It was made in 35 days.
Ewan was perfect for the part of Mark Renton.
However, he did have to lose two stones
and have his hair cut very short.

Trainspotting is a comic and tragic look
at the lives of a group of young Scots.
The four lads set out on a spree
of drug–taking and crime.

Ewan Bremner, Ewan McGregor, Jonny Lee Miller and Robert Carlyle in *Trainspotting*.

Trainspotting doesn't tell us
what's right and wrong.
It lets us make up our own minds.
It's dark and dirty, funny and sad.

Mark Renton is a junkie.
He tries to come off drugs without help.
At one point he goes head first
down a dirty toilet.
Ewan couldn't wait to stop filming that day.

Trainspotting was a big hit.
It made $70 million
and it made Ewan a star.
He was still very thin
when he married Eve, in France, in July 1995.

In the second half of 1995
Ewan made two more films.
The first was a mistake.
It was another costume drama
called *Emma*.
Ewan said 'I was terrible'.

He tried harder with his next film
called *Brassed Off*.
It tells the story
of the struggles of a brass band
in a Yorkshire mining town.
Ewan even played the French horn.
He was back on form.

6 Hollywood

Ewan's next job was nappy changing.
In February 1996
Eve gave birth to a little girl.
They called her Clara.

By the summer of 1996
Ewan was off to the US.
He wanted to try his hand at a Hollywood film.
The film was called *Nightwatch*.
Ewan played a killer.

He was given star status in Hollywood.
He had a big trailer
and a limo to drive him everywhere.
He enjoyed that
but he didn't enjoy the Hollywood film industry.
Ewan said 'I don't like it there'.

Ewan and Eve in October 1998.

In 1996, he took his family to Ireland
where he made his next film.
It was called *The Serpent's Kiss*.
Filming was relaxed,
so it give him time with Eve and Clara.

After that he had the energy
for two more films.
The first was a very small film
called *Swimming With Fishes*.
It was filmed in five days
in a fish and chip shop at the seaside.
Then it was back to the US
with the *Trainspotting* team
to make *A Life Less Ordinary*.

A Life Less Ordinary
is about a Scotsman
who is a bit of a drifter.
He kidnaps a woman and falls in love.
When it came out in 1997 it flopped.
People wanted another *Trainspotting*.
It made less than $10 million –
not a lot in the film world.

While he was in the US
Ewan had a part in *ER*.
He is a fan of the TV hospital drama.
After filming he was called back to London
for his own hospital drama.
Little Clara was very sick.
It was a very stressful time
for Ewan and Eve.

7 Star Wars

When Clara was better
Ewan started work
on the first of four films of 1997.
He starred in *Velvet Goldmine*.
It is the story
of the ups and downs of a 70s' Glam Rock band.
Ewan's childhood dream of being a rock star
was played out in this film.

On the first day of filming
Ewan had a phone call.
He was told he had a part
in the new *Star Wars* film.
He couldn't tell anyone.
He had waited 20 years for this job.

Ewan with his mother Carol at the London premiere of *Velvet Goldmine*.

George Lucas was making
three new *Star Wars* films
to show what happened
before the three earlier films.
Ewan was given the part
of Obi-Wan Kenobi.

The films tell the story
of Luke Skywalker's father, Anakin Skywalker
and how he turned into Darth Vadar.

The first of the three films is called
The Phantom Menace.
It was a difficult film for Ewan.
Often he had to act to thin air.
The special effects were put in later.
It was still a dream come true for Ewan.
When it came out in May 1999
it was the film everyone wanted to see.
He said it was 'magic'.

When the filming of *The Phantom Menace*
was finished in North Africa,
Ewan went back to England.
He went to the seaside
to make *Little Voice*.
It's the story of a shy woman
who wants to be a singer.
She makes it
with the help of her friend,
played by Ewan.

He was happy
to be playing a real person again.
After filming he took up motor bike racing.
Ewan has had a bike since he was a teenager.
His first bike was a Honda 100.
He now has four bikes
including a Ducati and a Triumph.

Ewan McGregor and fellow actor Charlie Boorman launched their own motorcycle team sponsored by BT Phonecards.

8 Natural Nylon

Ewan's last film of 1997
was called *Rogue Trader*.
It is the true story of Nick Leeson.
He was a trader working for a bank.
Then the bank went bust,
and Nick Leeson went missing.
So did £925 million of the bank's money.
Leeson ended up in jail for fraud.

Ewan and his friends
decided to start their own film company
called Natural Nylon.
He asked his Mum
to help him with his fan mail.

Later, Ewan went back to North Africa
for a short holiday
and to do the re-shoots
for *The Phantom Menace*.

In 1998 he went to Canada
to make a thriller about a female killer.
It was called *Eye Of The Beholder*.

Then he was off to Ireland again
to make a Natural Nylon film
called *Nora*.
It's the story of a lady called Nora –
the wife of the well-known writer,
James Joyce.

Just when it looked as if he would take a rest
Ewan went back to the stage.
He played the part of an art student
in the play *Little Malcolm*.
The play was directed by his Uncle Dennis.
He was paid just £250 a week.

The force is with Ewan McGregor.
Even when he crashed a 1100cc bike
he had only cuts and bruises.
The bike was a write off.

There seems to be no stopping Ewan.
As he says 'I can't say no'.
Ewan has lots of work in the pipe line.
He might make a film about John Lennon.
He might make a film in French.

Whatever happens,
Ewan is sure to be on
our screens for a long time.
Crieff is famous for Rob Roy
and now it's also famous for Ewan McGregor.